920

$\#4506$

Bowman, Kathleen

AUTHOR

New Women in Medicine

TITLE

new women in medicine

by kathleen bowman

Creative Education / Childrens Press

Published by Creative Educational Society, Inc.,
123 South Broad Street, Mankato, Minnesota 56001.
Copyright © 1976 by Creative Educational Society, Inc.
International copyrights reserved in all countries.
No part of this book may be reproduced in any form
without written permission from the publisher.
Printed in the United States.
Distributed by Childrens Press, 1224 West Van Buren Street, Chicago, Illinois 60607.
ISBN: 0-87191-508-1

Photo Credits:
Siecus: pp. 4, 5, 6; UPI: pp. 9, 30, 26; Ordean Torstenson: pp. 11, 12, 13
Tom Gill: pp. 14, 17, 19, 36, 39; Reni Photos: pp. 20, 23; Georgetown University: pp. 25, 29
Leslie Faricy: pp. 33, 35; Gordy Erspame: p. 43; Robert Crum: p. 47

Design concept and cover by Larry Soule

Library of Congress Cataloging in Publication Data
Bowman, Kathleen.
New women in medicine.
SUMMARY: Brief biographies of seven notable women
in the medical field: Elisabeth Kübler-Ross,
Kathryn Nichol, Anna Ellington, Estelle Ramey,
Mary Louise Robbins, Margaret Hewitt, and
Mary Calderone.
1. Women in medicine—Biography—Juvenile literature.
[1. Women in medicine. 2. Medicine—Biography]
I. Title.
R692.B68   610'.92'2 [B] [920]   76-4918
ISBN 0-87191-508-1

NEW WOMEN IN MEDICINE

Mary Calderone

It was a familiar event, in New York in 1915, to see Dr. Leopold Stieglitz making rounds in his old Franklin car. But one day he acquired a companion — a lanky young girl who bounced along beside him as they talked over the care of his patients. Her name was Mary Steichen, and she had come to live with the physician's family while she attended school in New York.

Mary was only eleven years old, but already she had seen much of the world. The daughter of photographer Edward Steichen, Mary spent the first ten years of her life in France. Visitors to the Steichen home often had famous names — Isadora Duncan, Brancusi, Rodin — and Mary delighted in the laughing and talking their appearances produced.

But life had its darker side, too. World War I broke out, forcing the Steichens to flee France and come to the United States. Soon after, her parents divorced, and Mary found a new home with the Stieglitz family.

Excited by her first-hand view of medicine with Dr. Stieglitz, Mary decided that she wanted to become a doctor. And everyone who knew her provided encouragement. What could possibly stop this exceptional young girl with so many talents — languages, music, acting, writing? It seemed that she could do anything she chose.

But the road to her goal was marked by many twists and turns. Mary found that her schooling was not nearly so exciting as the real world of doctors and patients. At Vassar College, she enrolled in pre-medical courses. But by the time of her graduation, she was so bored with scientific subjects that she decided to go on stage instead of to medical school.

But the stage, too, proved disappointing. For three years, Mary studied dramatics but could not perform well enough to satisfy herself. She later explained, ''I gave up acting when I found I wasn't good enough. You see, I was ambitious, and if I couldn't be as good as Katherine

4

Cornell — that is, tops — I decided I wouldn't go on with it."

Mary's unsuccessful stage career marked the beginning of a tragic period in her life. She was married in 1926, but the relationship ended six years later in divorce. Wearing hand-me-downs, Mary went to work in a department store to support herself and her two daughters. But it wasn't long before one of the girls died of pneumonia, and Mary's life seemed shattered beyond all repair.

Fortunately, she turned to a psychiatrist for help. This doctor, who later became her friend, assisted Mary in regaining her self-confidence and determination. So at the age of 30, Mary Calderone returned to her original childhood goal: to become a doctor.

Doubts plagued her nonetheless. Medical schools might not accept a single, 30-year-old woman with an eight-year-old daughter. And she herself wondered if her personal responsibilities would interfere with the difficult medical training period.

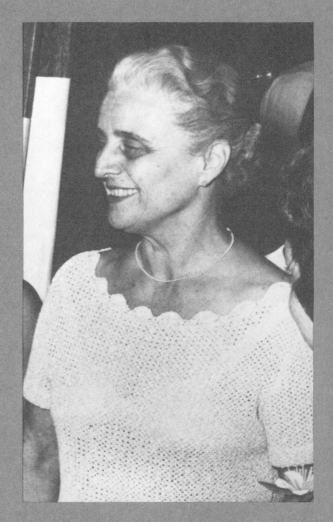

Mary, however, was accepted by the University of Rochester Medical School. She then faced the problem of obtaining the best care for her daughter, Linda. During the first two years of medical school she kept the child with her and employed a housekeeper. A young teacher lived with them to share expenses. But for the long hours of the third and fourth years of medical school, as well as for the internship, Linda went to the East Coast to stay with one of her mother's friends.

After finishing medical school in 1939, Mary decided against specializing in a particular field. That would have meant continued separation from her daughter. Instead, she got a fellowship from the city of New York to work in the area of public health at Columbia University. During this two-year program, she became close friends with Dr. Frank Calderone, a physician and New York City health officer. Eventually they were married, and at age 37, Mary began her second family.

Under happier circumstances, Mary Calderone again left medicine. By the time she was 42, she had two more daughters and chose to stay home with them until they were in school. Today Mary says, "My memory is of intense joy that, at my age, I could still have the pleasure of bearing children, nursing them, and caring for them personally and entirely during their infancy and early childhood."

While her children were small, Mary worked a few hours a day as a school physician, but she did not regard this as a "job." Her husband was now the chief officer of the World Health Organization, and those days were filled with travel, guests, and maintaining a large house. She recalls, "I knew that eventually I would go to work sometime, but . . . this was the period I was known as 'Mrs. Calderone,' and people barely remembered that I, too, was a physician."

Not until she was 50 years old (the same year that her husband retired) did Mary Calderone accept her first full-time job — as Medical Director of the Planned Parenthood Federation. Although many physicians in 1953 considered the position a dead-end, Mary viewed the situation as ''the right person for the right job at the right time.'' In a world with exploding populations and dwindling resources, she thought that family planning was becoming a major social responsibility as well as an individual right. Her stage experience and her enthusiasm combined to make her an extremely effective speaker, and opportunities for public appearances rapidly increased. Before long, Mary Calderone had achieved wide recognition for her work in birth control.

But over the years Dr. Calderone became deeply troubled by many of the letters she received at Planned Parenthood. They were often filled with fear and guilt and ignorance about sex. She was especially concerned about young people who were caught in the midst of changing rules of behavior.

Following a 1961 conference on church and the family, Dr. Calderone and five other participants decided to form SIECUS (Sex Information and Education Council of the U.S.) Its aim was to educate people toward healthy sexuality by providing information in the forms of workshops, materials, and training sessions. Mary left her position with Planned Parenthood to become the Executive Director of SIECUS.

SIECUS' services have been so well-received that Mary Calderone, now 70, travels an average of 50,000 miles a year. She often speaks several times a day to teachers, parents, ministers, and women's groups, and also appears on radio and TV. And she is pleased by the young people she sees — by their openness to facts and by their view of sex as something that involves trust and responsibility.

Those who see Mary Calderone cannot help but be impressed by her vigor,

her honesty, and her sense of purpose. Focusing her blue eyes intently, she says, ''Sex involves something you are, not just something you do. Children and adults must be taught to understand their sexuality so they can respect it, appreciate it, and use it properly at the right time in life.''

For Mary Calderone, there was a long, bumpy road between those first exciting days with Leopold Stieglitz and her current successes. But despite the most bitter tragedies and frustrations, she has never given up, never stopped growing. A silver-haired great-grandmother steadfastly pursuing her goals, Mary Calderone stands today as an inspiring model to other women, both young and old.

Kathryn Nichol

It was a busy morning at the Dean Clinic in Madision, Wisconsin. Doctors' schedules were filling up fast. In the pediatrics department, a nurse picked up the phone. "Pediatrics. May I help you?"

"Yes," replied a young mother. "I'd like to bring my son in this morning. He has a fever and sore throat."

"We're booked solid for the morning. Oh, wait — Dr. Nichol could see him. She has an opening at eleven o'clock."

"Oh . . . it's a woman. Tell me — is she any good?"

When the nurse reported the mother's reaction, Kathryn Nichol was not surprised. She has learned that as a woman physician she must often prove her competence in new situations, whereas male doctors are usually accepted automatically. But these experiences have not made her bitter.

"The key is to turn these obstacles into positive experiences," Dr. Nichol believes. "Many people have never seen a woman doctor. Once they know me and trust me, they look back on their initial doubts with embarrassment. For many it is the first time they see the unfairness in their judgments of women. That's important."

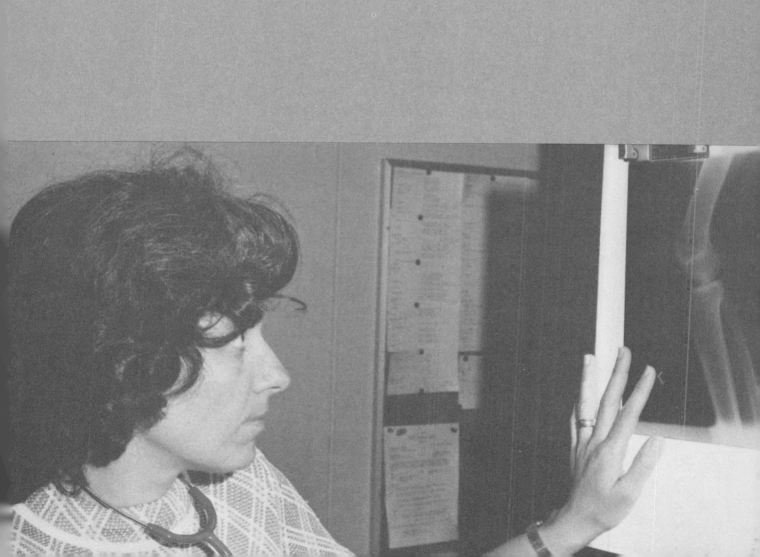

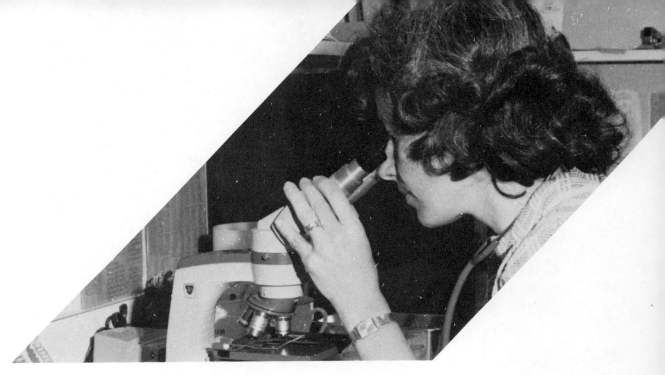

A busy pediatrician with three young children of her own, Kathryn Nichol finds that her multiple roles of doctor, wife, and mother enrich one another. Her brown eyes light up as she explains, ''Going home from the clinic with a sense of accomplishment, I am able to bring freshness to wifehood and motherhood. And it works the other way, too. I've become a much more understanding doctor since I've been a mother. I've felt myself the panic of having a tiny infant with a high fever in the middle of the night. That's made a real difference in my reactions to parents with sick children.''

As a pediatrician, Kathryn Nichol treats children from birth to adolescence. As well as seeing the usual variety of ailments afflicting this age group — from broken arms to earaches — she is constantly facing the unpredictable: a case of child battering, a diagnosis of leukemia, a birth disorder. And she is emphatic about one thing: emotional needs are as real as the physical ones. Dr. Nichol believes she must be the source of information and reassurance to both the child and the family members. She says, ''My commitment is to the very best care I am able to give — and that means giving something of myself, not just a prescription to take to the drugstore.''

Becoming a doctor was Kathryn Nichol's goal for as long as she can remember. Her mother was a nurse, and young Kathryn pored over her mother's medical textbooks with great interest. Both parents were supportive of her decision to become a doctor, although her father withheld his encourage-

12

ment until he was satisfied that she knew what the choice involved. Kathryn recalls, ''He kept asking, 'Do you know how long it will take? Do you really think you have the self-discipline?' But once he knew I had considered these questions, he was totally enthusiastic.''

Dr. Nichol remembers her first year of medical school at the University of Wisconsin as very discouraging. ''I thought we were going to learn how to take care of people,'' she says now. ''But it turned out to be the same old routine of competing for good grades.'' The young medical student was so disheartened that she took a part-time job in a doctor's office. This work kept her in touch with the actual practice of medicine and provided the encouragement she needed to continue in the more academic setting.

Discouraging too were the reactions of her friends to the fact that a female would choose to go to medical school. ''People either put me on a pedestal or told me I should be home where I belonged. It was such a hassle that I began to tell people I met that I was a home economics major instead of a medical student. Luckily, I think those kinds of prejudice are disappearing now.''

Was the struggle worth it for Kathryn Nichol? ''Definitely,'' she replies, waving to a young patient running past her office door. ''There's nothing in the world like kids. Caring for them and their families is the most gratifying work I can think of. I wouldn't want to be doing anything else.''

13

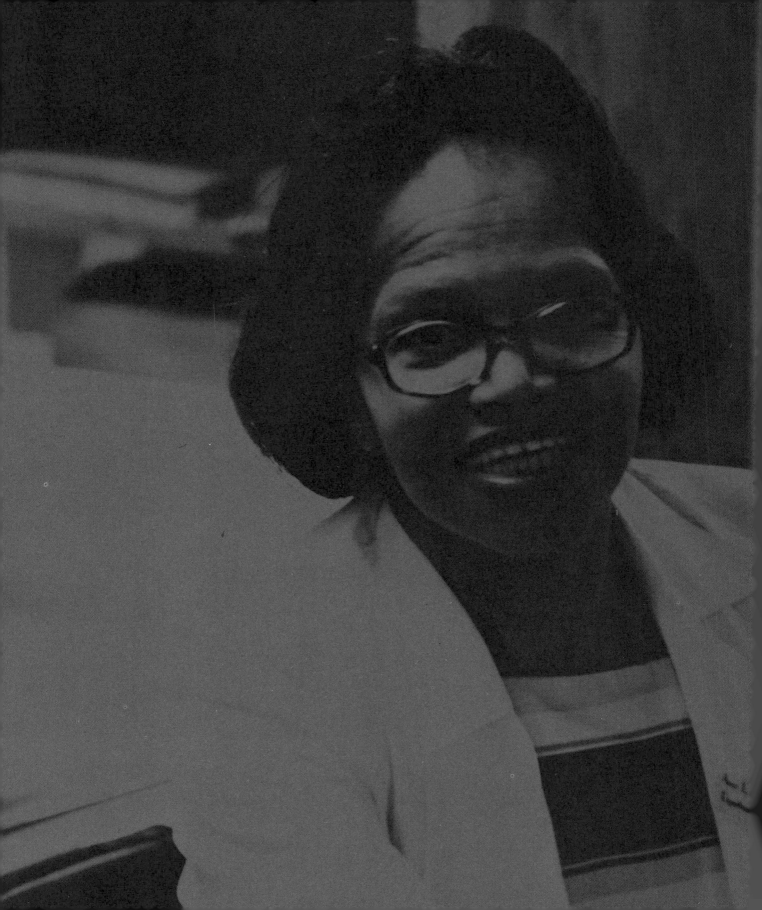

Anna Ellington

''Paging Dr. Ellington . . . Dr. Anna Ellington, please call the Emergency Room at once . . . .''

Anna Ellington was just leaving the hospital after a long day when she heard the page. Rushing to the nearest phone, she dialed the Emergency Room. The pediatrician on call answered. ''Anna, a six-year-old boy just came in — aspirin overdose. Seems to be in a coma. We've got to do an EEG right away. Can you stay to read the results?''

''Of course. Let the technician know we're coming. I'l be down to see the outcome in a few minutes.''

Dr. Ellington straightened her weary shoulders as she rode the elevator back up to her office on the fifth floor. ''Drug overdose,'' she thought, a frown crossing her face. ''Why can't people be more careful?''

Inside her office, Anna Ellington traded her trench coat for the familiar white lab coat. Then she called home. ''Hi, Frederick,'' she greeted her eight-year-old son. ''You and your father are going to have to get along without me for dinner tonight. There's a very sick child in the Emergency Room. I'll be home as soon as I can.''

Meanwhile, in the EEG laboratory, a technician placed electrodes on the scalp of the sick child, who lay pale and motionless on the examining table. These tiny receivers began to pick up the electrical activity of the boy's brain, and the medical team watched anxiously as the long needles zig-zagged back and forth across the recording paper. The needles' faint scratching was all that could be heard in the small, white room.

The test was nearly over when Dr. Ellington came through the swinging door of the laboratory. Everyone's eyes were fixed on her as she picked up the huge stack of paper that the machine had produced. They were waiting for Anna to read the ''language'' of the boy's brain waves and tell them his chances of recovering.

She opened out the huge accordion-like pages of the EEG ''record.'' Her face fell as she noticed a small number of waves per minute and areas where the peaks were flattened out. The pattern was typical of someone near death.

Turning to the pediatrician, Dr. Ellington said grimly, ''The chances of this child recovering are very slight. We need to repeat this test in the morning. Meanwhile, give him all the support you can — transfusions, a respirator, whatever is necessary.'' She paused to study the face of the sick boy for a minute, then left the room.

Driving home, Anna Ellington let out a deep sigh. Her thoughts were focused on two young boys — one lying near death in a coma, the other waiting anxiously for her at home. Each child represented two important worlds for Anna Ellington: the world of medicine and the world of her family. And sometimes, like tonight, she was torn by the feeling of being needed in both places.

16

17

"Maybe I should have been a mathematician after all," she mused. Sometimes that seemed less complicated. But she had decided against mathematics because, as her mother put it, "Your brother Henry's a mathematician. We've already got one of *those*."

"And I almost became a musician," she recalled. But her older sister had already become one of *those*. So Anna Ellington, a bright young girl from Birmingham, Alabama, went off to Oberlin College in Ohio to study chemistry. At the urging of her adviser, she decided to become a doctor. No one in her family had become one of *those*.

Curious about how the mind works, Anna became a special kind of doctor called a *neurologist* — one who cares for the brain and the nervous system. It was exciting, it was fascinating, and sometimes it was plain hard. Especially on nights like this, when she wanted to be caring for her patients and for her family at the same time.

As Dr. Ellington pulled into the driveway, Frederick came bursting through the door. "Hi, Mom!" he said, grinning.

"Guess what? I did the dishes all by myself."

"That's great, Frederick," his mother said, giving him a hug. As she watched him skip up to the door along side her, a vision of the pale child on the examining table crossed her mind — a painful contrast to her own lively son.

The lingering smells of dinner interrupted her thoughts as she entered the house. Anna Ellington suddenly realized she was hungry. And as she turned the corner into the kitchen, she saw her husband setting a place for her at the table — checkered napkin, bright blue placemat, and her favorite dishes. "Sit down and relax," he said. "I think I've managed to keep it all warm. . . . And by the way, the hospital just called. The boy with the drug overdose is showing some improvement."

Anna sat down to dinner, exhausted but happy. She was glad to be home and relieved by the news from the hospital. As she looked into the eager faces of her family and imagined the pale child laughing once more, she was certain of one thing. That being a doctor, a wife, and a mother was just exactly what she wanted to be.

19

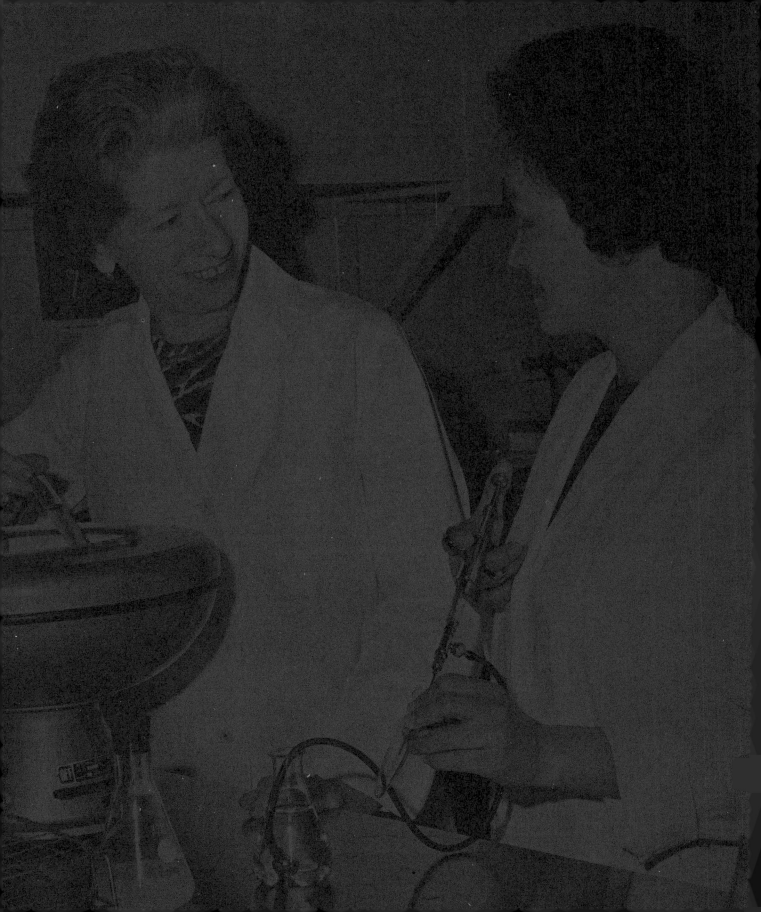

Mary Louise Robbins

''I was one of those kids who let caterpillars crawl up and down my arms and legs instead of running away from them,'' says Mary Louise Robbins. Her interest in biology began when she was just a small child. An avid collector of wiggly creatures, she would watch intently as the caterpillars slowly transformed themselves into beautiful butterflies.

Since those days, Mary Louise Robbins has dedicated her life to unravelling some of the mysteries of nature. She has turned her interests to studying, not caterpillars, but tiny organisms that most of us will never see — the viruses and bacteria responsible for infections, colds, polio, influenza, and maybe even cancer. ''It's truly amazing,'' she says, ''that these miniscule living things can do so much in so little time.'' And those of us who can remember our last bout with the flu are certain to agree with her.

The microorganisms (tiny living things) that Dr. Robbins studies may be small, but their effects have been tremendous. Microorganisms have been responsible for some of the most terrible epidemics in the world, including the yellow fever outbreak during the construction of the Panama Canal. And it is likely that viruses will be discovered as one of the causes of one of today's most feared diseases — cancer. These facts make the work of people like Mary Louise Robbins enormously important.

To study some microorganisms, Dr. Robbins often uses the powerful electron microscope, which can magnify a cell 100,000 times. She says, "realizing that you are looking at living creatures that small is a very exciting event." Also important in her laboratory are animals such as mice, rabbits, and guinea pigs; they make it possible for her to test the effects of vaccines that are developed to cure diseases.

It was not surprising that Mary Louise Robbins developed an interest in medical research. Both her great-great-grandfather and her great-grandfather were doctors. Her uncle, who taught at Harvard Medical School, was also a physician. Dr. Robbins today believes that this family history gave her the confidence to act upon her own interests in medicine.

After graduating from American University, she earned master's and doctor's degrees at George Washington University in Washington, D.C. The first woman in her family to enter the medical profession, she was also the first woman full professor on George Washington's medical school faculty.

But Mary Louise Robbins' life has extended far beyond the walls of her university laboratory and classrooms. She has served as a visiting scientist in such faraway places as Cairo, Egypt, and Baghdad, Iraq. But perhaps the most satisfying event of all was the year she spent in Japan. Captivated by its tea gardens, pagodas, and cherry blossoms, she fell in love with the long, mountainous country. And because she wanted to become as much a part of Japan's culture as possible, Dr. Robbins learned to speak Japanese, do flower arranging, and observe tea ceremonies.

During her stay in Japan, she worked side-by-side with some of the world's most advanced microbiologists, and it was there that she learned the use of the electron microscope. She found her colleagues so gracious that she plans to live permanently in Japan after she retires, editing Japanese science journals.

For Mary Louise Robbins, a career in medical research has meant not only finding causes and cures for human diseases, but also understanding the peoples and cultures of the world.

22

23

Estelle Ramey

One day in the summer of 1970, Estelle Ramey picked up a newspaper and was jolted by the headline, "DOCTOR ASSERTS WOMEN ARE UNFIT FOR TOP JOBS." She could hardly believe her eyes. Wasn't this the twentieth century? Who could be saying such a thing?

Reading on, she saw that Edgar Berman, famous physician and adviser to Hubert Humphrey, had made the statement. He had told a national Democratic committee that women are not suited for positions of leadership because of their "raging hormonal imbalances."

It so happened that Estelle Ramey was not only a woman, a doctor, and a leader — she was also an endocrinologist. For 25 years, she had studied exactly what Berman was talking about — bodily secretions called hormones and their relationships to stress and disease.

It was time, she thought, to step out of her secluded Georgetown University laboratory and into the turbulent world of public opinion. She agreed to debate Edgar Berman face-to-face in what came to be called the "Battle of the Raging Hormones." It was to be a turning point in the life of this witty, attractive scientist who until then had been little known outside of medical circles.

The crowd was buzzing with excitement as the two doctors entered the Madison Hotel in Washington, D.C. From the start, Estelle impressed the audience with her good looks, confidence, and logic. She began by observing that females are not the only people with hormonal disorders. Diabetes, for example, affects many more men than women — including many members of the U.S. Congress. Surely Dr. Berman would not want to remove these responsible men from their jobs, argued Dr. Ramey. And it made as little sense to suggest that hormones should keep women out of similar positions.

Before the debate, Dr. Berman had expressed his horror at the idea of a female President. He said that "raging hormones" would get in the way of her decision-making. "Would you have wanted a female in the White House at the time of the Bay of Pigs?" he challenged.

24

26

Dr. Ramey reminded him that the Bay of Pigs decision was in fact made by a male President with a hormonal disorder. John F. Kennedy was a victim of Addison's disease. Yet no one asked Kennedy to step down. No one challenged his decisions on the basis of hormones. Then why claim that a female cannot make decisions because of her hormonal make-up? It made little scientific sense, argued Dr. Ramey.

If anything, she maintained, hormones give women a slight biological advantage. It is common knowledge that women have a lower rate of heart disease and live longer than men. Researchers have found that this is because of a female hormone called *estrogen,* which slows down the aging of blood vessels. Male hormones, on the other hand, cause tissues to "burn out" more rapidly and are a major factor in high blood pressure.

Males' lives are put further in danger, said Estelle Ramey, by society's ideas of how they are supposed to behave. Men, for example, are expected to be unemotional and not to cry. "The code of the West has you riding off into the sunset with a stiff upper lip when you are defeated," noted Dr. Ramey.

Men are also under pressure to succeed, to produce, and to make all of the big decisions. Dr. Ramey explained, "Men have designed a society that's calculated to make it difficult for them to live to a ripe old age. And they insist on running it without any help from their natural partners — women."

But women, too, are handicapped by society's notions of how they must be. Often looked upon as irrational and

27

unstable, women are portrayed as "delightful little things who are just too frail to stand up to stress." As a result, they are not encouraged to use their talents. Even though the U.S. sends more women to college than any other country in the world, Dr. Ramey noted, "we have the lowest percentage of practicing women attorneys, doctors, chemists, engineers and physicists of any industrial country." Dr. Ramey herself is part of a meager 4% of female full professors. "They're going to put me in the Smithsonian when I die," she added with bleak humor.

In the end, our society suffers a tremendous loss of creativity, pointed out Dr. Ramey. She said, "As an example, you might ask if we might not by now have developed a cure for cancer if we had developed the talents of all our geniuses."

Her suggestion? "Stop wasting those women's brains and in the process stop wasting the lives of the overworked American man."

Estelle Ramey seemed to have won the "Battle of the Raging Hormones" hands down. But winning a debate is not her real goal. She views the rights of women as a cause which is part of the struggle for *human* development. She seeks better lives for both women and men and objects to competitiveness between them. "You don't have to be one-up so that somebody else is one-down," she declared.

How did Estelle Ramey herself overcome the pressures that discourage many women from careers?

She gives credit first to her parents, from whom she gained unshakable self-confidence. Dr. Ramey recalls that her mother "believed I was a unique human being, and there was nothing I couldn't accomplish."

Influential too has been her husband, James T. Ramey. Even though Estelle Ramey was almost done with her Ph.D. degree at the time of their marriage in 1941, she planned to give it up to become a full-time wife and mother. But James urged her to continue, saying, "I can't live two lives for both of us." He perhaps feared that the talented young woman would soon become bored — a condition which Estelle Ramey now sees in many American women.

So when James Ramey accepted a job in Knoxville, his wife applied for a teaching position at the University of Tennessee. But the chairman of the chemistry department curtly told Estelle that he had never hired a woman and would *never* hire a woman. He told her to go home and take care of her husband.

29

30

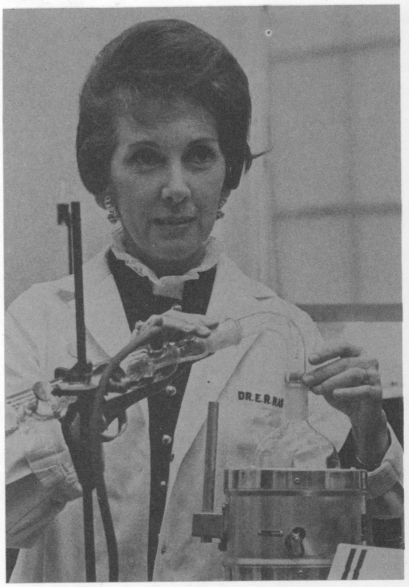

But World War II broke out soon afterward, and men in the department were called into the military. Swallowing his pride, the chairman called Estelle Ramey and offered her a job, saying, "Mrs Ramey, it is your patriotic duty to teach!" Estelle continued teaching and doing research through the war and through the birth of two children.

When James Ramey joined the Atomic Energy Commission in Chicago, Estelle enrolled in the University of Chicago Medical School. There she earned her doctorate and did research in endocrinology. Since 1956, she has been on the staff of the Georgetown University Medical School. She continues her research and also teaches medical and dental students.

Since her debate with Edgar Berman, Estelle Ramey has continued to be an active and visible public figure. Energetic, witty, and well-informed, she is asked to speak to many political and educational groups throughout the country. She has also written for popular magazines, such as *McCall's* and *Ms*. In her efforts to promote a fuller life for both men and women, she continues to be supported by her husband. Estelle's office bookshelves contain a picture of James with the following inscription: "To Stella, my not-so-silent partner. With great admiration, James."

At 56, Estelle Ramey is dramatic proof that the essential feature of "new women" is not youth, but their spirit and sense of purpose. Estelle Ramey dreams of the day when men and women work together cooperatively. She pleads, "Let us share the work. Each of us has only a short span and each of us wants to get as much out of life as we can. That's what it's like to be a human being. Not a man. Not a woman. A human being."

Margaret Hewitt

''OK, Nancy. Remember to take a deep breath with this next contraction. You're doing beautifully . . . the baby should be born any time now.''

The calm, dark-haired woman speaking in reassuring tones to the expectant mother is Margaret Hewitt, nurse-midwife. One of her hands is on the mother's stomach, timing the contractions that will push the baby through the birth canal. The other clasps the mother's hand in a gesture of support and companionship. Surrounding the mother-to-be are her husband and two other nurse-midwives, assisting Margaret with the delivery.

But delivering the babies is really only one part of her job. Before the birth, she spends many months talking with the mother and father, hoping to prepare them for their new responsibilities. She also teaches them about the care of newborn babies. And after they leave the hospital, Margaret often visits the new family at home to see how they are getting along.

32

34

"We try to give emotional support as well as physical care. That's really important in setting a positive tone for a new family. Good nurse-midwives are usually good at providing comfort and companionship."

Her small, strong hands forming circles as she talks, Margaret Hewitt gives the impression of having thought a lot about her work. And it's a special kind of experience for her. "There's nothing quite like hearing a baby give out its first cry," she says thoughtfully. "It's a happy time for everyone."

Margaret stretches wide and yawns. "I've been up most of the night," she explains. "Sometimes when the phone rings I think, 'Oh, no . . . .' But the minute that human being is on the other end of the line everything changes. I've got all the energy in the world."

She glances at her watch. "You'll have to excuse me now. I want to stop by to see Nancy and John and the new baby on my way to the clinic." And suddenly she is out of the overstuffed chair, striding down the hall in her white sneakers.

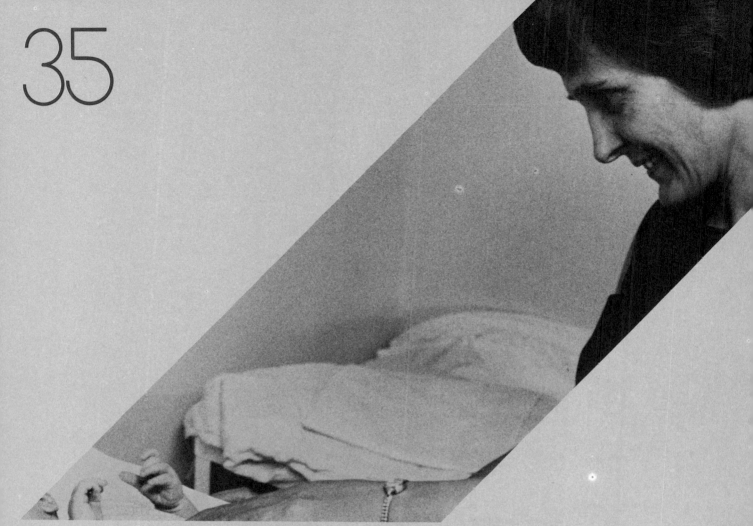

From time to time Margaret adjusts her stethoscope so that she can listen to the baby's heartbeat. Her blue-gray eyes light up above her hospital mask as she catches the pulsating sound. She passes the instrument to the mother so that she can hear for herself how strong and healthy her baby is.

Suddenly Nancy's eyes close as she feels another contraction coming. "Take a deep breath, Nancy," reminds her midwife. "That's it . . . . . Now push — keep pushing — that's right. Good." Margaret Hewitt has left the mother's side to prepare to deliver the baby's head. "I think one more good contraction is going to do it." Margaret smiles up at the mother and father. They are totally absorbed in the act of delivering their first child.

As another contraction begins, Nancy's eyes open wide. She senses that her baby is about to be born. "Take a deep breath, now. Good. Push — push — keep pushing . . . ." Nancy is raised to a near-sitting position by her husband and the other nurse-midwives so that she can watch her infant

36

being born.

"OK," says Margaret. "Here comes the baby's head — what a lot of dark hair! Push steadily now — there!" Nancy groans with exhaustion from the work of delivering the baby's head, but a smile flashes across her face as she beams up proudly at her husband.

"OK — the shoulder now," Margaret continues. Nancy bears down once more, and suddenly Margaret's hands are expertly helping a squirming red baby scream its way into the world.

"It's a girl!" everyone cries out in near unison. The excitement escapes no one. Margaret is now calmly, but swiftly tending to the small infant. She clears out its nose and throat. Then she places it, still wet and wriggling, onto the mother's stomach while she cuts and ties the umbilical cord. Nancy beams at her new baby — checking out every detail. Ten fingers, ten toes, her father's ears. The infant's black hair is still matted and clinging to the top of her tiny head. "Look, her eyes are open," notices her father. "She's going to be a pretty one."

37

An air of celebration takes over the room, and Margaret comes around to give Nancy and her husband a hug. She picks up the baby and smiles at it, saying, ''Well, you're a lot bigger than we thought you'd be.'' Then she gives the infant to another nurse-midwife, who checks its reflexes and breathing.

''A pediatrician will be in later to do a more complete examination,'' explains Margaret. ''But she certainly seems like a perfect one.''

''Can the baby stay here?'' Nancy asks.

''Oh, yes. This is your room — for the whole family.'' Nancy looks around the room, seemingly aware of it for the first time, though she has been there for nearly six hours of labor and delivery. Spacious and colorful, the room has easy chairs, lamps, and several pictures on the wall. It is a cheerful place for a new family to spend its first hours together.

''Margaret . . .'' begins Nancy, grabbing the nurse-midwife's hand. ''I want to thank you . . . it was fantastic. Not at all what I imagined a few months ago.''

''You did most of it,'' Margaret replies softly. ''You and John. If I do my job right, that's just the way it should be.'' And she excuses herself, leaving the new family with a few moments alone.

39

40

Margaret checks her watch. In another hour she must be down in the clinic to meet a new expectant couple who have chosen to have their baby delivered by a nurse-midwife. But she takes time now for a break and to talk about her job.

Slumping into a big overstuffed chair, she pulls her feet up under her. Her desk is covered with a wide array of objects: a few baby toys, a stray knit cap, and stacks of medical journals. On the wall are framed diplomas from Columbia University and the American College of Nurse-Midwives.

"I suppose most people still think of midwives as delivering babies on kitchen tables in the hill country of Tennessee," she muses. "But now most midwives are highly trained members of modern, big-city hospitals."

Margaret is enthusiastic about the teamwork between nurse-midwives and obstetricians (doctors who specialize in delivering babies.) "Obstetricians are usually overworked," she explains. "They must try to divide their time between deliveries, office visits, surgery, and emergencies. They sometimes can't be with a mother through the whole delivery even though they want to be. So we handle most of the normal cases, staying with the same couple from their first clinic visit through the delivery. This frees up the doctor to take care of emergency situations. It works out very well."

Like many of today's nurse-midwives, Margaret Hewitt started out as a registered nurse. She became more and more interested in mother-child health. "So when I went back for more schooling," she explains, "I thought it would make sense to be trained as a midwife, too." At Columbia University, she learned to care for women from the first days of pregnancy through the delivery — providing everything remains normal. Nurse-midwives are trained to be alert for complications and to call in a doctor should any problems develop. Since her training, Margaret Hewitt estimates that she has delivered hundreds of babies.

41

Elisabeth Kübler-Ross

''There!'' The pale, pajama-clad boy tossed down his crayon and thrust his picture into the hands of the doctor seated beside his hospital bed.

''Thank you, Jimmy,'' responded Dr. Elisabeth Kübler-Ross. As she studied the drawing, the boys' eyes — large and feverish against his thin face — were fixed on the small, bespectacled woman physician. She had become an important person to this six-year-old dying of leukemia. He had spent most of the past year in the hospital, and it was lonely. But Dr. Ross's visits often brightened his day. She seemed to understand how much he wanted to be out riding his red two-wheeler like the other kids in his neighborhood.

As Dr. Ross looked at the drawing, she saw that Jimmy had colored in a huge black military tank. Standing right in front of its barrel was a tiny human figure holding up a stop sign, as if to prevent the ugly machine from crushing him.

Dr. Ross studied the boy's face. It wore an expression mixed with fear and anger. Picking up a crayon, she began to work on the picture herself. She drew in a second small stick figure with his arm around the person Jimmy had drawn.

When she handed the picture back to Jimmy, he looked at it eagerly to see what she had added. He turned his face up to Dr. Ross, and this time Jimmy managed a weak smile. Dr. Ross put her arm around

his shoulders and smoothed his blond hair, now patchy from the effects of large doses of medicine. "I'll be back a bit later," she said. "And I really like those pictures."

As Dr. Ross walked down the hospital corridor, she thought some more about Jimmy's picture. It told her that he knew he was dying and was angry and afraid. He imagined death to be a terrifying destructive machine that would overpower him — much like the tank he had drawn. He wanted to stop it, but felt as helpless as the tiny stick figure holding up the sign.

Dr. Ross knew this was a stage in Jimmy's acceptance of his death. It was normal for him to feel angry and afraid. So she expressed her companionship and support by adding to the drawing and by touching the dying child. She hoped that he would pass through his anger eventually and be more at peace with himself.

Elisabeth Kübler-Ross's major goal as a physician is to help patients through what she calls the ''stages of dying.'' First there is disbelief that we may actually die. Then anger — ''Why did it have to be me?'' After a time of sadness and depression, there follows acceptance.

Dr. Ross has found that people who are dying, as well as their families, go through these stages. Her job is to provide support and comfort for people as they pass on their way to what she hopes is a peaceful death.

Jimmy was able to do just that. Several weeks later, Dr. Ross visited Jimmy to find that he had completed another drawing. This time it was a large black bird in flight — but the tip of its upper wing was colored as golden as sunlight. When she saw this drawing, Dr. Ross knew that Jimmy had now accepted the fact that he was going to die.

Elisabeth Kübler-Ross is pleased when she is able to successfully help patients work through their feelings about death. But she has found that in our society many things get in the way of accepting death.

One of these obstacles seems to be our preoccupation with science and technology. Attempts to prolong a person's life at all costs with machines and complicated devices often mean that a dying patient does not have his or her feelings recognized. Dr. Ross explains, ''He may cry for rest, peace and dignity, but he will get infusions, transfusion, a heart machine . . . . He may want one single person to stop for one single minute so that he can ask one single question — but he will get a

44

dozen people round the clock, all busily preoccupied with his heart rate, pulse . . . his secretions or excretions — but not with him as a human being."

Afraid of death themselves, the hospital staff often pay attention to the equipment rather than to the patient. Like most of us in America, they have grown up shielded from death and afraid of confronting it. Perhaps you yourself have heard people say, "No, Janey isn't going to Grandpa's funeral. It would be too much for her." Or perhaps you have gone to the hospital to visit a sick friend or relative only to find that you weren't allowed past the lobby.

The result is that most Americans grow up to pretend death doesn't exist, says Elisabeth Kübler-Ross. The old, sick, and dying are sent off to nursing homes or hospitals where we needn't face them. There, such patients lead a lonely existence, lingering on from visiting hours to visiting hours.

And when the death of a friend or relative finally occurs, we avoid that too. Dr. Ross describes a kind of drive-in funeral home which is becoming popular in the United States. "You drive up in your sports car, look through a glass window, sign a guest book, and take off." This, she says, is a way of denying that human beings die. It would be better, she believes, if people would talk about death as a part of life, just as when a woman is expecting a baby. Dr. Ross insists, "Death belongs to life as birth does."

Swiss-born, Elisabeth Kübler-Ross's life has caused her to regard death differently from most people in this country. One of her first confrontations with death on a large scale was in World War II concentration camps, where she did relief work. She believes this experience ex-

45

46

plains part of her concern with death and dying.

But her insights into American attitudes toward death seem to come mainly from her comparison of the attitudes with those in Switzerland. There, she notes, people die differently — at home, surrounded by friends and loved ones and a familiar environment. Children are present, which prepares them to face death as a natural part of life when they become adults.

After several years of observing attitudes toward death in this country, Elisabeth Kübler-Ross decided to act on her concerns. When a group of University of Chicago students came to her in 1965 for help with a study of people facing death, she decided that the patients themselves would be the best teachers. She set out to find patients to converse with. But no one could understand why she would want to talk to dying people. Many doctors and nurses thought the patients would be disturbed by frank conversations about death.

Finally, she was given the chance to see one patient. As it turned out, the man was extremely grateful to talk to someone about his feelings. He also felt useful again, in the belief that his efforts would help others.

As a result of this experience, Elisabeth Kübler-Ross began a series of seminars on death at the University of Chicago's Billings Hospital. In each seminar, a patient was invited to talk about his or her feelings and thoughts in this human crisis. In the audience were doctors, nurses, orderlies, ambulance drivers, and members of the clergy — all hoping to learn to work better with the dying.

Today, Elisabeth Kübler-Ross carries on her work, but she is no longer associated with a clinic or university. She is now an international consultant who conducts seminars and workshops in the care of the sick and dying. In the last five years, she has given approximately 700 such presentations. She is grateful to her husband, also a physician, and her two children for helping her keep such a busy schedule.

A small woman with wispy hair, Elisabeth Kübler-Ross holds an audience spellbound with stories of real patients and their struggles to accept death. But the aim is not only to learn to help the dying, she stresses. The lessons are for the living. She says, "It is from our dying patients that we learn the true values of life, and if we could reach the stage of acceptance in our young age, we would live a much more meaningful life, appreciate small things, and have different values."

47